The

DIGITAL
TRANSFORMATION

Cookbook

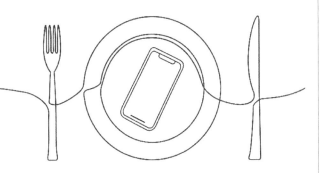

How to transform your people,
process, and data

MAULIK SHAH

The DIGITAL TRANSFORMATION Cookbook

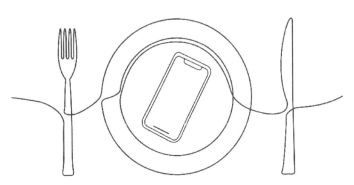

Table of Contents

Foreword 7

Ch. 1: Understanding Digital Transformation 15

Ch. 2: Drivers for Digital Transformation 25

Ch. 3: Technologies Powering Digital Transformation 35

Ch. 4: Roadmapping Your Digital Transformation Strategy................. 47

Ch. 5: Leading Your Team Toward Digital Transformation 59

Ch. 6: Companies Leading Digital Transformation Today...................... 69

Ch. 7: Delivering Success Through Digital Transformation 83

Conclusion... 95

Worksheet... 99

Endnotes 109

About The Author............................ 117

About Invonto 119

TO ALL BUSINESS LEADERS

TRANSFORMATION IS POSSIBLE

Foreword

Since the early 1990s, we have been witnessing a digital revolution that is transforming our world. Much like the industrial revolution, the digital revolution requires companies to rethink their business, how it delivers value to their customers, and what its future looks like. The process that an organization goes through to adopt digital technologies and change its workplace culture is what I refer to as digital transformation.

In many ways, the current digital revolution is similar to the American Industrial Revolution of the late 1700s and early 1800s. The industrial transformation required organizations to update their physical infrastructure, refine manufacturing processes, and retool employees. Similarly, digital transformation requires organizations to update their IT infrastructure, automate their business processes, and train their employees to work with new digital tools. The outcome of both revolutions remains almost the same — an investment in technology that results in more efficient businesses, happier customers, and more profitable ventures.

The difference between the digital revolution and the industrial revolution is that digital transformation doesn't require organizations to upend everything they have in place to make room for newer technologies, tools, and processes.

With digital transformation, organizations can start with small low-risk initiatives that limit disruption during day-to-day operations. A carefully executed digital strategy will help organizations prioritize and address all of its digital needs to achieve a successful transformation.

The key to digital transformation success is a constant evolution in how your organization operates and takes advantage of new digital technologies. For the most part, companies have relied on web-driven digital solutions for automation. However, in recent years, digital technologies for cloud, mobile, Internet of Things (IoT), and artificial intelligence (AI) have rapidly advanced. These technologies offer tremendous opportunities for companies to rethink existing business models and find technological solutions to existing business problems.

While digital technologies have proven beneficial across industries, not all businesses have started their journey towards a transformation. There are three common reasons organizations resist change: they don't know where to start, they assume change will be costly, and/or they're simply not aware of the resulting benefits. Based on my 20 years of industry experience, the businesses that commit to change are the ones that grow the fastest and improve their brand value the most.

The decision of whether or not to go digital is an easy one. Just look at the successful organizations and upcoming startups in your industry. What fuels their success?

Usually, the answer lies in their digital adoption — whether a business is going through a digital transformation or born digital. Organizations can be separated into four categories based on their path to digital adoption:

Digital Native: Organizations that are founded through modern digital technologies and are revolutionizing fundamentals of business models in their industry.

Early Adopters: Established organizations that are actively experimenting with and implementing new digital technologies to keep up with the evolving business landscape.

Slow Adopters: Established organizations that are delaying the implementation of new technologies until after these technologies have delivered proven benefits within their industry.

Benchwarmers: Established organizations that are actively discussing digital technologies, but have yet to implement any. Some have disregarded advancements in technology entirely.

COMPANIES WHO ADOPT DIGITAL TRANSFORMATION

DIGITAL NATIVE	EARLY ADOPTERS
UBER	Walmart
AirBNB	Marriott
Amazon	Pepsi
Warby Parker	Starbucks
SLOW ADOPTERS	**BENCHWARMERS**
Macy's	JCPenney
Best Buy	Toys R' Us
J. Crew	Sears
GNC	Kohl's

Where does your business fall on this spectrum? How far along are you in your digital transformation journey? Are you actively implementing digital solutions, or are you just now learning about the gradual benefits of the latest technological advancements? What roadblocks are you facing in going digital?

In this book, I'll be discussing the importance of digital transformation, the current state of digital, and what organizations need to define a successful digital transformation strategy for all their business initiatives.

My goal is to help you get started on this journey. Similar to how a recipe cookbook offers step by step guidance on preparing a meal, this book will provide you with step-by-step guidance on how to define, design, and initiate digital transformation for your organization.

Digital transformation is a shift in mindset that requires organizations to rethink their business strategies, products, and operations.

The Digital Transformation Cookbook

Chapter 1

Understanding Digital Transformation

At its core, digital transformation is the integration of modern technologies into every area of a business, resulting in a radical change to how an organization operates and delivers value to its customers.

However, digital transformation isn't just about technology; it's an evolution of your business, your people, and your culture. It's a mindset shift that requires organizations to rethink their business strategies, products, and operations. In a way, digital transformation is business transformation.

THE BUSINESS VALUE OF DIGITAL TRANSFORMATION

Digital transformation enables organizations to improve in three key areas of their business: employee satisfaction, client relationships, and innovation. It is so critical to the economic success of a company, in fact, that CEOs are now including digital transformation strategies as part of their overall strategic plans. More than 75% of business leaders surveyed in a McKinsey research study believe that the digital economy offers significant growth opportunities for their companies. What's more, according to a spending report from the IDC, organizations worldwide will spend over $2 trillion on digital technologies by 2022.[1]

Digital transformation fosters innovation at every level of a business. Through digital transformation, enterprises can offer exceptional and personalized customer experiences in every aspect of the customer journey, which leads to increased brand loyalty and customer retention. The automation of business processes improves operational efficiency and boosts employee job satisfaction, while the ability to collect digital data makes it possible to analyze trends and improve business performance through data-driven decision making.

The rapid development of digital technologies and digitally-driven product lifecycle management processes has accelerated the pace at which organizations deliver new products and services. In the digital age, organizations are required to think outside of the box. New digital technologies provide opportunities to refine existing business models and overcome growth barriers.

Digital transformation benefits all organizations regardless of their size, industry, products or services. While digital transformation for larger organizations is often a lengthy process that requires C-suite buy-in, the result is usually hyper business growth. And for smaller organizations where digital transformation is simpler to implement, the result could prove game-changing, making them far more competitive.

"Through digital transformation, enterprises can offer exceptional and personalized customer experiences in every aspect of the customer journey, which leads to increased brand loyalty and customer retention."

SUCCESSFUL EXAMPLES OF DIGITAL TRANSFORMATION

Digital transformation may feel unattainable. You might be asking yourself; how can my organizations guarantee success? While success is never guaranteed, many organizations are already benefiting from their digital transformation efforts. Let's explore some real-world examples:

Domino's Pizza – To improve the customer experience, Domino's developed a digital platform that lets customers place pizza delivery orders online, through mobile apps and even on Twitter. Domino's is using voice recognition to automate pizza orders made via telephone. Dom, Domino's AI assistant, can take orders and notify customers where their pizza orders are in the delivery process. Domino's president and CEO said the company aims to one day be "100% digital" with additional ordering and in-store technology.[2]

Putnam Investments – Putnam, a provider of retirement services, mutual funds, and institutional investment, has moved many legacy applications to the cloud and is focusing on process automation. Putnam has also created a data science center that uses machine learning to develop more significant business insights to provide better customer service.[3]

Cemex – In 2017, the global building materials company began leveraging digital technologies to position itself as a leader in the building materials supply industry. Cemex launched Cemex Go, a digital customer integration platform that includes web and mobile applications designed to improve customer engagement with a seamless experience for order placements, live shipment tracking, contract agreements, and invoice management. The app suite has completely changed the way customers interact with Cemex products and services, and has allowed Cemex to meet customer needs efficiently. Additionally, Cemex launched Cemex Ventures, a venture capital unit tasked with fostering construction innovation by working with startups, entrepreneurs, and industry leaders.[4]

There are several other successful examples of digital transformation in practice, which I will discuss more in chapters six and seven.

GET STARTED WITH A DIGITAL TRANSFORMATION STRATEGY

If you are interested in beginning the process of digital transformation, start by defining your strategy and goals. A successful digital transformation strategy means you MUST:

- *Define your business goals*
- *Get commitment from leadership*
- *Communicate your goals to the entire team*
- *Experiment with smaller projects to demonstrate success*
- *Find the right technology partner(s) for your initiatives*
- *Inform your workforce of the upcoming changes*

To succeed, you must evolve by focusing on business results, innovation, and continuous improvement.

By developing a digital transformation strategy, you will define new ways to create, monetize, and increase value, so you get a competitive edge over your business rivals. If you do not address these needs, you will fall by the wayside.

"The last ten years of IT have been about changing the way people work. The next ten years will be about transforming your business."

- Aaron Levie, CEO, Box

Consider the many retailers that have shut down because they couldn't compete with other digital-native or transformed businesses. Retailers like Toys 'R Us, JCPenney, Bed Bath and Beyond, Borders, and Kohl's have succumbed to the rapid rise of Amazon with some barely staying afloat.[5] Contrast this to businesses like Walmart and Best Buy that have invested in innovation and successfully carved out an audience for themselves. Future-minded companies are in a unique position to benefit significantly from digital transformation before it becomes widely adopted.

Now that you understand what digital transformation is let's talk about a few ways digital transformation can benefit your business.

Access to valuable data insights breeds smarter businesses that make better decisions which leads to hyper business growth.

Chapter 2
Drivers for Digital Transformation

New digital technologies are transforming the fundamentals of business in every industry, forcing organizations to take a holistic view of their business models and processes. Organizations that transform their business operations with new technologies will thrive in the digital age.

This is not an overnight change—it is an ongoing process that requires you to transform, measure, and oversee technology advancements.

Most digital transformation efforts fail due to an inadequate budget,

KEY DRIVERS OF DIGITAL TRANSFORMATION

Data Source: Altimeter

lack of management commitment, and a resistant workplace culture.[6] A successful digital transformation starts with a well-defined strategy that prioritizes initiatives, sets goals, and identifies the criteria for success. With a plan in place, digital transformation can provide numerous benefits that will make the transition worth the time and effort.

"In today's era of volatility, there is no other way but to re-invent. The only sustainable advantage you can have over others is agility, that's it. Because nothing else is sustainable, everything else you create, somebody else will replicate."

- Jeff Bezos, Founder of Amazon

We'll talk more about how to ensure a successful digital transformation strategy in chapter four. Now, let's dive into some ways digital transformation can revolutionize your business.

IMPROVING THE CUSTOMER EXPERIENCE

Digital tools and technologies are part of our daily lives. According to a study by We Are Social, there are 5.11 billion unique mobile users in the world today.[7] We rely on our gadgets for everyday functions, such as shopping, banking, traveling, entertainment, and even making our homes "smarter." You must have heard the phrase, "There is an app for that." Whether you want to pay bills, shop, get food delivered, book travel, buy movie tickets, or control thermostats in your home, you can do it all using a mobile or cloud app.

As a customer, we've grown to expect companies to provide interactive and meaningful ways to benefit from their products and services. Oracle's CEI report revealed that 86% of consumers would pay more for a better brand experience. It also revealed that 89% of consumers would gladly work with a competing brand following a poor customer experience.[8] Within the next few years, there will be a whole new generation of customers who will spend their money only on the companies that offer quality digital experiences.

Customer retention is a key driver for transformation, and having an engaged customer helps organizations gather valuable insights from customer data. This data can be vital for business success. For that reason, the customer experience must be at the core of any organization's digital transformation.

The success factors in customer experience transformation include:

- *Designing personalized customer experiences*
- *Digitizing customer journeys*
- *Achieving customer adoption of digital customer journeys*

New digital technologies create functionalities to help you acquire, retain, and assist customers, while at the same time enabling you to save money. Customer experience improvements often lead to new and innovative solutions that create additional value for the business. The efforts of customer experience improvements can yield high returns.

FOSTERING COLLABORATION

At times when there is a shortage of skilled labor, and when organizations are desperately looking for ways to improve employee productivity, automation through digitization can help them retain and attract talent. With digital transformation, you can automate critical areas of your business, such as sales and field service operations, plant operations, back-office administration, inventory management, and customer service operations. Automation reduces manual efforts so employees can focus on more essential tasks. As a result, automation enhances employee productivity and job satisfaction, and improves their value to the business.

The digital workplace centers around your employees' ability to communicate, collaborate, and connect with other employees across departments. Cloud, mobile, IoT and augmented reality applications make it easier for geographically dispersed teams to work together. API integrations enable data sharing across systems in real-time. A truly collaborative environment improves employees' understanding of the entire business and makes business more scalable.

ENABLING DATA-DRIVEN DECISION MAKING

A non-digital organization faces three main challenges with their data:[9]

- *Collecting data from multiple sources with no real-time tracking*
- *Exposure to data security and compliance threats*
- *Translating data into actionable business insights*

Digital transformation can help you overcome these challenges by making data accessible and centralized. Additionally, data analytics gives you valuable insights into customer preferences and buying behaviors, which you can use to deliver better products, personalized services, and targeted promotions.

Access to valuable data insights breeds smarter businesses that make better decisions—and that leads to hyper business growth.

BOOSTING YOUR COMPETITIVE ADVANTAGE

To remain competitive, grow, and evolve, it's imperative that you adopt new digital technologies. A 2017 study by SnapLogic concluded that companies are losing $140 billion annually in wasted time, resources, duplication of effort, and missed opportunities. The losses are in large part due to legacy infrastructure that is limiting accessibility to critical company data.[10] Businesses that continue to rely on legacy systems risk losing customers to their digitally-enabled competitors.

Digital transformation allows you to operate more efficiently, retain and grow your customer base, find new opportunities, and increase revenue. To benefit from digital transformation, you must bring your people, processes, and data together to create value for your customers and maintain your competitive edge.

In the next chapter, we will discuss the technologies that will help transform your business into a digital enterprise.

In this digital era, you can't afford to maintain the status quo. Technological debt will greatly impact companies that reject the idea of digital.

Chapter 3

Technologies Powering Digital Transformation

The launch of the world wide web in the early 1990s gave way to the digital revolution that we are experiencing today. In the last 30 years, many technological advancements have emerged in the areas of hardware, software, and networking. Fortunately, over time the processes to build digital solutions have matured and costs associated with the hardware and network bandwidth have lowered. With the availability of cloud-based infrastructure, organizations do not require significant investments to procure and manage hardware equipment. This has lowered the barriers for digital adoption.

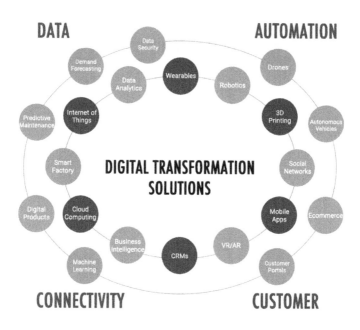

On the other hand, the rapid advancement of digital technologies means you need to evolve constantly. Those that reject the idea of digital transformation will continue to accrue "technological debt," which will eventually make it difficult for them to stay competitive.

To flourish in the digital age, it is critical that you analyze the changes required in your existing business models and implement digital technologies that drive value for your business. Let's take a look at the most commonly used digital technologies.

CLOUD COMPUTING

Organizations promoting a collaborative work environment need business applications that can be used by geographically dispersed teams. Many of these organizations rely on on-premise software and IT infrastructure to run their business operations. However, on-premise infrastructure limits the usage of enterprise software within an organization's private network. These legacy systems make it difficult for organizations to share their software solutions with customers and business partners. As a result, growth demands are not met and innovation is prohibited. Cloud computing solves these issues efficiently and has become a high-demand solution over the last decade.

Cloud is a metaphor that refers to servers, databases, software applications, networking, and file storage that is accessible through the Internet. It enables process automation and IT modernization, which are key business drivers.

Cloud-based applications and infrastructure offer flexibility and scalability while lowering up-front costs and increasing reliability. Public cloud service providers, such as Amazon Web Services, Microsoft Azure, and Google Cloud, do not require businesses to invest upfront in expensive IT hardware. The pay-as-you-go model gives organizations the flexibility to scale IT operations up or down to meet growth demands, or lack thereof. Most organizations are moving IT to the public cloud as part of their digital transformation initiatives. In recent years, large enterprises are even implementing multi-cloud infrastructures to manage workloads more efficiently, make IT operations more scalable, and distribute outage risks.

In addition to its cost benefits, cloud technologies offer businesses expansive value. To start, organizations can more efficiently meet customer and employee demand for high-end digital products and improve accessibility to services. Additionally, cloud technologies make it easier to refactor, upgrade, and integrate existing siloed applications, and also quickly build new digital services.[11]

In the workplace, cloud applications foster a flexible and collaborative work environment that allows employees to work remotely. This leads to greater efficiency and retention among the workforce.

Cloud-based applications can help you catapult toward digital transformation and rapidly meet business objectives, consumer expectations, and employee requirements.

MOBILE APPLICATIONS

A study conducted by the Pew Research Center revealed that 81% of U.S. adults have a smartphone—up from 35% just eight years ago when Pew conducted the first survey. As the number of mobile users—and the time they spend on their mobile devices—increases, mobile must be at the forefront of your business strategy.

Mobile apps make your business and products more accessible to customers, increase engagement, and help build brand recognition. They also make it easier for employees to manage their job functions when working remotely. When combined with artificial intelligence, internet of things, and augmented reality, mobile technologies give you the tools that simplify many business processes, such as reading sensory data, operating equipment, simulating training, and tracking people and equipment.

Mobile apps are now a necessity for businesses to attract new customers and retain employees. The next generation of customers and employees will be digital-native, with a greater familiarity of touch screen devices. According to a McKinsey survey, more than 77% of CIOs are considering a mobile-first approach for digital transformation.[12]

"At least 40% of all businesses will die in the next 10 years, if they don't figure out how to change their entire company to accommodate new technologies."

- John Chambers, Executive Chairman, Cisco Systems

ARTIFICIAL INTELLIGENCE, MACHINE LEARNING, AND DATA ANALYTICS

Artificial intelligence, the machine emulation of human intelligence and processes, has become an essential part of accelerating business growth. With enterprise solutions like cognitive computing, machine learning, deep learning, robotics process automation, and data analytics, AI allows you to deliver personalized experiences to customers based on their past behaviors, create conversational experiences such as chatbots, and implement image recognition solutions for your business.

Today machine learning solutions are helping organizations solve their most complex business problems. By enabling process automation, predictive maintenance, personalized experiences, and data-driven decision making, machine learning can help your business build digital products that meet customer needs, prevent issues, reduce waste, and improve sustainability.

Data is at the center of digital transformation. Every digital organization collects a massive amount of data from customer interactions, employee activities, and equipment. With data analytics, organizations can unlock insights from all data types to improve business processes, forecast trends, and identify growth opportunities.

Data analytics delivers the real benefit of digital transformation, giving digital organizations an edge over their non-digital competition.

INTERNET OF THINGS (IoT)

Ever use an Amazon Alexa or Google Home? You just benefitted from the internet of things. IoT helps connect people, equipment, and data for enabling process automation. According to Gartner, there will be more than 20 billion connected devices by 2020.[13] While a majority of IoT implementation has surrounded consumer applications, like smart home solutions, IoT can have a significant impact on industrial automation.

Sensors on industrial equipment, tools, and transportation systems can automate industrial processes by providing control to remotely access, operate, and maintain. IoT helps improve the efficiency of industrial equipment and people on the job function.

IoT devices collect massive amounts of data, and businesses are now starting to understand how valuable this data is. With data insights, organizations can track equipment, monitor equipment health, offer

predictive maintenance, and gather usage details. Organizations are using this data to streamline workflows, improve existing products, and introduce new products.

AUGMENTED AND VIRTUAL REALITY

The impact of augmented reality (AR) and virtual reality (VR) is resonating across several industries, especially in the areas of:

Training and Simulation: AR and VR enable IT to retool high-cost training and simulation environments (i.e., manufacturers can reproduce maintenance and repair scenarios in virtual environments).

Field and Customer Service: Virtual solutions let remote experts to see what field technicians see and so they can offer guidance as maintenance or mechanical tasks are performed.

Communication and collaboration: AR and VR provide IT with opportunities to change how your business, as well as your employees, share information and take action. For example, engineering teams can implement VR to collaborate in real-time, enabling them to test and refine their designs. Marketing managers can use AR to view retail shelf inventory and sales data.

Brand promotion: With immersive AR experiences, marketing teams can engage with customers, promote marketing campaigns, and boost brand recognition.

In this digital era, you can't afford to maintain the status quo. To grow and gain a competitive advantage, it's critical that you transform your operations ahead of your rivals, especially as these processes and applications become digital-centric.

In the next chapter, we'll discuss how to roadmap your digital transformation strategy to ensure the success of your digital transformation efforts.

Having a strategic digital roadmap is the key to enabling change in a coordinated and effective manner so you can generate the value your company expects.

Chapter 4

Roadmapping Your Digital Transformation Strategy

A digital roadmap is a blueprint of your digital transformation strategy. It is a high-level document for outlining your business objectives and an actionable plan for your digital initiatives.[14]

Previously, we examined the digital transformation technologies organizations can leverage to grow. Now, let's explore how to roadmap your digital transformation strategy.

DIGITAL TRANSFORMATION ROADMAP

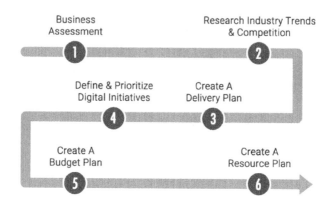

STEP 1. BUSINESS ASSESSMENT

To prepare for your digital transformation, start with a detailed assessment of your current business. Understanding your organization's strategic goals, key performance indicators (KPIs), and growth opportunities in your sector can help define your business needs. Be thorough in this initial assessment so that you can identify problem areas that are slowing or prohibiting your growth. By focusing on improving or eliminating these problems, your organization will discover dramatic growth opportunities and may expand products and services.

Here are a few questions to ask yourself as you assess your business:

- *What aspects of your business are running optimally? What can be improved?*
- *Are your employees productive and motivated? What feedback have they provided about the business?*
- *Are your customers happy and satisfied with your products and services? Have you identified specific pain points?*
- *Are your competitors investing in technology? If so, what are the results of those investments?*
- *Does the introduction of new technology create new opportunities for your business?*
- *What is your projected business growth rate over the next year? The next five years? The next ten years? Will you be able to achieve the projected growth rate with the existing systems and processes?*

STEP 2. RESEARCH INDUSTRY TRENDS AND COMPETITION

Researching industry trends and assessing your competitive land-scape can help you identify both opportunities and threats. Start your competitive research by studying what your top three competitors are doing, or have done, to address the challenges you have identified in your business. Additionally, research what innovative solutions they are building to fuel their business growth. Prepare a worksheet to compare data across multiple competitors.

While doing thorough competitive research, be sure to look beyond just established companies. Digital-native startups have become a disruptive force in many industries. For example, consider the impact of Airbnb in hospitality and Uber in transportation. Not only have they disrupted their respective industries, but they also redefined those industries, their products, and how they service customers.

Don't forget to look outside of your industry as well. Every industry is aiming to evolve in line with the changing requirements of its customers to deliver innovative new services and improve its internal processes. By observing how companies in other industries are leveraging new technology, you can expand your insights and increase your profitability in the long term.

A competitive analysis will help you understand the market, identify experiences customers are seeking, and find opportunities to build a thriving business.

STEP 3. DEFINE AND PRIORITIZE DIGITAL INITIATIVES

Since digital technology affects every organization differently, you need to define where change is needed the most in your business (i.e., operational performance, customer engagement, creating new digital products and services). If you develop a clear point of view on the opportunities or risks in each area, you can discover which capabilities you need to focus on.

Each digital initiative might differ in terms of its scope, resource requirements, development process, and impact on the business.

Consider prioritizing your initiatives based on their value, impact, and effort needed to achieve the desired outcomes. Start with simple but high impact projects to secure quick wins. Instead of building full-scale solutions, you can create an MVP (minimum-viable-product) with essential features. Experimenting with MVPs allows you to test a solution's viability before fully committing to it.

"It's no longer the big beating the small, but the fast beating the slow."

-Eric Pearson, CIO, International Hotel Group

STEP 4. CREATE A DELIVERY PLAN

Successful transformation requires buy-in from all stakeholders, including leadership, employees, customers, and business partners. Communicating the vision for your digital transformation (i.e., what it looks like and why it's important to the organization) is critical for receiving buy-in from stakeholders. A vision that's clearly stated and resonates with all stakeholders will also keep them on your side when you hit some rough patches. Your goals and priorities might change based on the feedback received from the stakeholders.[15]

Your delivery plan should also include the scope for each digital initiative, communication plan, resource requirements, development process, criteria for measuring success, and a governance policy. If you've built digital solutions before, you may already have the tools and processes in place that you can leverage. However, be sure to evaluate these to ensure they are a fit for new initiatives. If you have never built a digital solution, you'll want to research tools, technologies, and processes for your projects. Before you jump into the development stage, identify the development and delivery processes to ensure you have standard practices in place for your entire organization.

Some of your transformational initiatives can break down into smaller projects to address their various change requirements. For example, maybe your digital initiative is to automate your sales operations. On the software side, this means having a mobile application for the sales team in the field, a back-end system for data storage, and APIs for transferring data to and from the mobile app. On the hardware side, it means procuring the mobile devices with adequate network bandwidth for the field users. You will also need additional IT infrastructure for the data storage and back-end application. Each one of these can turn into an individual project and require a designated team. The functional requirements of a digital product can also separate into multiple milestones. Setting milestones can help set stakeholder expectations for when a change will apply to their working environments.

Digital transformation can be a daunting undertaking without proper planning. But with stakeholder buy-in and a thorough delivery plan, you'll be well on your way towards achieving your business objectives and becoming a digital enterprise.

STEP 5. CREATE A BUDGET PLAN

The spending associated with digital transformation may seem over-whelming for any business, but the risks an organization faces from digital competitors are much more significant. Organizations that are on the fence with their digital adoption carry huge technological debt and lack automation needed to run an efficient business. These organizations will have to increase their spending on digital technologies over the next few years to keep up with the digital revolution.

Creating a budget plan requires a clear understanding of the scope for each initiative. You should also have a buffer in your budget for project risks and scope changes. Your budget plan should have a contingency to account for new technology innovations that might require further modifications to your digital products or render your current investments obsolete.

Inadequate funding is one of the main reasons why digital transformation initiatives fail. Therefore, it's imperative that you allocate the proper funding for your digital transformation.

STEP 6. CREATE A RESOURCE PLAN

Technology is not the only cost associated with digital transformation. As you begin your digital transformation journey, it's crucial that you build a team with the right skills and mindset to put your strategy into action. Start by conducting an assessment of the capabilities of your team. If you identify skill gaps, you'll have to either train your current staff on the new requirements or hire.

Roadmapping Your Digital Transformation Strategy

For many organizations, digital transformation is a daunting undertaking. They've been hyper-focused on their business, while ignoring the evolving world of digital technologies. Even for the organizations with exposure to digital technologies, the rapid advancement in cloud, mobile, IoT, augmented reality, virtual reality, and artificial intelligence has made it challenging to employ the required skills needed. While it's not difficult to transform one process on your own, transforming your entire business is an entirely different matter. That's why many organizations turn to technology vendors—to help alleviate the stress inherent in developing digital transformation initiatives while reducing the long-term fixed costs associated with acquiring different skill sets.

While a large-scale digital transformation can be over-whelming, having a strategic digital roadmap will help you approach change in a coordinated and effective manner so you can generate the value your company expects.

Instilling a digital culture in your organization means that everyone in the company understands the impact digital can have on work environment, customer relationships, and the quality of products and services.

Chapter 5

Leading Your Team Toward Digital Transformation

Digital transformation is more about a culture change than it is the adoption of digital technologies. It affects how your employees manage their job function, and changes how your customers, suppliers, and business partners interact with your business. The success of your digital transformation is dependent on buy-in from these stakeholders. While having a plan will help you communicate your strategic objectives, you'll need to take a step further to get full support from your team.

ESTABLISH DIGITAL LEADERSHIP

Digital transformation touches on almost every aspect of your business. Consider assembling a core digital transformation team that includes representation from each area of the business. This team will be responsible for the successful execution of your digital initiatives, the administration of your governance policy, and the reporting of results to stakeholders.

"You can't delegate digital transformation for your company. You and your executives have to own it! Executives need to engage, embrace and adopt new ways of working with the latest and emerging technologies."

-Barry Ross, CEO and Co-Founder, Ross & Ross International

Additionally, you may want to assign a Chief Digital Officer (CDO) to lead this team.[16] CIOs typically concentrate on IT services that keep the company running efficiently and with little disruption. The CTO focuses on using digital technologies to promote a specific digital initiative. However, digital transformation requires a completely different skillset—transforming processes and developing new business models. That's where the CDO comes in. This executive will oversee both strategy and execution of the organization's digital goals, incorporate new objectives in the strategy, and stay on top of new industrial developments, and incorporate new objectives in the strategy. The CDO will also ensure that the organization is receiving the desired benefits from their digital transformation objectives.

GET YOUR TEAM ON BOARD FOR DIGITAL TRANSFORMATION

Implementing new digital solutions and overhauling your business processes alone will not result in a successful transformation. After all, digital transformation is all about improving employee and customer experiences. You cannot define an effective digital strategy with your end-users on the sidelines. You need to engage your stakeholders early in the process.

To ensure buy-in from your employees and customers throughout your transformation you must:

- *Get employee and customer input while defining user journeys and experiences.*

- *Demonstrate completed product features as early in the process as possible.*
- *Deliver quality products and offer training to onboard new users.*
- *Seek feedback and incorporate that in future product releases.*

Instilling a digital culture means that everyone in your organization understands the impact digital can have on the work environment, customer relationships, and the quality of products and services. Consider establishing product committees for individual digital products to solicit ideas and create a sense of ownership amongst the stakeholders. Establishing ownership will help you deliver the best possible employee and customer experiences and make user adoption smoother. Mass user adoption is critical for maximizing a return from your technology investments and further growth of your business.

"Instilling a digital culture means that everyone in your organization understands the impact digital can have on the work environment, customer relationships, and the quality of products and services."

CULTIVATE A CULTURE OF INNOVATION

If you want your team to commit to the mission, give them the space to innovate. According to a study by Gallup, only 29% of workers surveyed strongly agreed that they were expected to be creative or thinking of new ways to complete work.[17] Companies that place too many restrictions on the process of innovation will only hamper creativity and the possibility of success. Giving employees the freedom to ask questions and seek solutions outside of past limitations will help plant the seeds of innovation. Organizations should encourage their teams to examine every possible solution to the problem. Allow them to experiment and test various technologies throughout the process.

Do not forget that failure is a crucial part of digital transformation. Digital transformation does not promise an immediate solution; instead, it provides a means to experimentation that will enable successful innovation.

PUT DATA AT THE CENTER OF DECISION-MAKING

Every digital transformation initiative should begin with data. Data is the foundation that allows you to understand the current state of your business and make informed decisions to help you achieve your desired business outcomes.

"Data is the foundation that allows you to understand the current state of your business and make informed decisions to help you achieve your desired business outcomes."

For your digital transformation to succeed, you need access to clean and consistent data across every system and channel. The ability to review your organization's performance in real-time is necessary for making the most out of your digital transformation initiatives.

INVEST IN EMPLOYEE TRAINING

Whether you outsource your digital transformation or do it with internal teams, you will be changing your business processes and workflows through the introduction of new technologies. This abrupt change will impact everyday job functions of all your employees. For seasoned employees, it might be more difficult for them to learn new processes. You will need to invest in employee training so that your valuable employees can transition from outdated processes to the new ones.

With digital transformation, you will break barriers between departments. Your employees may find themselves closely integrated, and this will require additional training so that employees understand the operations of other departments. By cross-training employees, you can expect greater consistency, improved business efficiency, and increased employee satisfaction.

START SMALL AND GO SLOW

Digital transformation will impact all areas of your business. Some companies make the mistake of introducing several changes simultaneously. An overwhelming amount of changes can be disastrous and completely ruin any chance of a successful transformation. I recommend that you start with incremental changes to ensure that your business continues to operate normally. By using this approach, you will be able to measure the effectiveness of each new change accurately and compare the results to your digital roadmap.

Businesses who prioritize their objectives will be even closer to achieving their transformation goals. Many enterprises have applied everything I've spoken about thus far to succeed in their transformation efforts. In the next two chapters, we will take a look at a few key examples of successful digital transformation.

Integrating technology to enhance the customer experience gives companies the opportunity to meet user needs, add more value, and increase revenue growth.

Chapter 6

Companies Leading Digital Transformation Today

Now that we have explored the concept of digital transformation at length, it's fair to ask, "what does digital transformation look like in practice?"

While the concept of digital transformation is relatively new, there are already several digital transformation examples that showcase how a company can successfully elevate itself.

WALMART

The retail giant, Walmart, is another prominent brand investing in digital transformation. After seeing the threat Amazon posed to smaller retailers, Walmart is positioning itself as a worthy competitor by improving front-end and back-end technologies to drive efficiency.

Walmart has several initiatives in progress to create a frictionless shopping experience. They first started building their tech division, now called Walmart Labs, in 2011 with a few key acquisitions. In 2016, Walmart purchased e-commerce giant, Jet.com, for $3.3 billion. Walmart entered a five-year deal with Microsoft to focus on digital advancement, technology upgrades, and delivering new and essential customer experiences.[18] Additionally, Walmart pushed for greater collaboration between the e-commerce and tech divisions. The result has been several improvements to internal operations and customer services.

Walmart has ensured their employees have the right tools to deliver the best customer experience. The introduction of scannable employee badges allows employees instant access to crucial information like staff schedules, product availability, and promotions. Electronic shelf labels are improving the price accuracy and availability of product information. Walmart has also launched 17,000 virtual reality training devices for employees.[19]

Customers are reaping the benefits of Walmart's digital transformation investment. The retail brand announced free next-day delivery offerings without membership, a direct jab at Amazon, who was promoting free next-day delivery to Prime members.

Walmart also launched grocery curbside delivery services that have boosted sales by 37%.[20] Walmart's website and mobile apps make it easy for customers to make purchases and pick them up without entering the store. Walmart is further investing in this service in a few ways.

One store is testing a giant robot tasked with storing up to 4,000 crates of groceries for customer pick-up.

Elsewhere, the company is planning on fulfilling grocery deliveries with autonomous vehicles.

Going forward, Walmart is investing heavily in blockchain, though it's too early to tell what the high-level strategy will be.

BEST BUY

If you were asked about Best Buy five years ago, you might have said it was on its deathbed. Today, Best Buy has gone on a digital transformation journey that has made it a legitimate Amazon competitor.

Since Amazon's rise to prominence, Best Buy was often called "Amazon's Showroom." Most customers would look at products at Best Buy and then make purchases on Amazon's website. The foot traffic was high, but the sales were not matching.

Best Buy realized they needed to compete with Amazon's low pricing. To improve its financial position, the company launched a strategic plan called "Renew Blue," which called for strengthening relationships with vendors, revamping stores, increasing same-store sales, eliminating unnecessary costs, and ramping up its online business. They accomplished this by reducing costs by $400 million in first-year, closing under-performing stores and improving the supply chain.[21]

"Our purpose is to enrich lives with the help of technology. Make a big difference in peoples' lives by addressing key human needs, whether it's entertainment, productivity, communication, food preparation, security or health."

-Hubert Joly, CEO, Best Buy

Next, Best Buy invested heavily in their application development. The company runs all its development for BestBuy.com, Best Buy Canada, and Best Buy Mexico through its Seattle office. They built a private cloud network that allows them to optimize their web and mobile assets and produce digital media assets.

The investment in digital technologies allowed Best Buy to extend its online sales distribution network with its ship-from-store concept, which it has now rolled out to 1,400 store locations. Best Buy's network allows over 70% of U.S. customers to reach a store within 15 minutes of their location.[22] Store accessibility enables the company to invest in digital solutions to improve in-home services like GeekSquad and offer them to their local customer base.

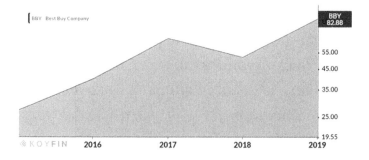

Through its transformation, Best Buy is estimating $50 billion in revenues and $1 billion in cost savings by 2025.[23] By investing in technology to provide better customer services, Best Buy has outlived expectations and has put a dent in Amazon's e-commerce empire.

WEIGHT WATCHERS

Founded in the 1960s, Weight Watchers has been a leading fitness brand for over 50 years. The company focus has always been about weight loss. However, disruptive startups, wearable devices, and consumer mobile apps in the health space caused the decades-old brand to lose its luster.[24] The company felt that it needed to reposition itself as a brand focused on overall health and wellness to better address customer needs.

In 2015, Weight Watchers set a goal to become the leading business for digital experiences in weight loss. Before it could achieve that goal, it needed to access its current digital infrastructure. Weight Watchers relied on legacy applications that prevented it from scaling the business or deploying new features. The website was updated a few times a year with long downtimes. Things weren't much better on the mobile front, with a mobile app that had abysmal ratings and poor user experience.

To deliver on their promise of focusing on health and wellness, Weight Watchers invested heavily in developing a new website and mobile app with microservices designed to meet customer needs. The website is now capable of pushing regular updates seamlessly within a few minutes, with no downtime. The new Weight Watchers mobile app introduced new features, such as the ability to scan barcodes at the supermarket for updated nutritional information about each product and track food consumption and weight loss in real-time. The application then used this data to create a personalized fitness program for individuals. Weight Watchers has also invested in unique partnerships with Headspace and Aaptiv to deliver high-quality digital content to its customer base through the mobile app.

These partnerships and updates have resulted in stronger user reviews, an increase in engagement, and has even earned a Webby award.[25]

The next phase of Weight Watcher's digital trans-formation journey plans is, in part, to focus on voice search. Voice search is growing in popularity with readily available personal assistants like Amazon Alexa. Weight Watchers is launching Wellow, a voice search application that will integrate with popular personal assistants to deliver the same value through this new technology.[26]

STUBHUB

StubHub set out to become a leading ticket exchange with ambitions to take down Ticketmaster. With cons-umers moving to the convenience of online ticket sales, StubHub had a unique opportunity to gain ground on Ticketmaster.

StubHub's strategy was to focus on the customer experience. To meet customer needs, StubHub invested in automation and cloud solutions to improve the online buying experience.[27] The StubHub website processed payments quickly, even with dramatic traffic spikes. Key vendor partnerships enabled StubHub to reduce image load times on their content-rich website by six times. StubHub also invested in the mobile experience and developed integrations with social channels, like Facebook.

The mobile app also shows users the 360-degree view from available seats in real-time with webVR and 3D models.[28] Users can put the phone on a VR headset to get a much more immersive experience in making seat selection.

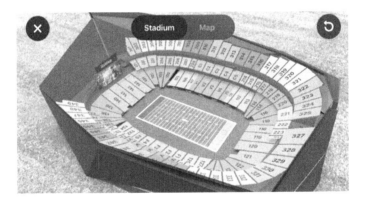

The various investments provided users with an excellent experience that promoted trust and resulted in an increase in ticket sales.

MARRIOTT

In the era of Airbnb, Marriott is creating value by leveraging digital solutions to deliver extraordinary experiences for its customers worldwide. Marriott has successfully used technology for learning, engagement, and sharing across its 30 brands—not an easy feat to achieve. It did this by addressing customer pain points through a variety of tech innovations.

The Marriott mobile app has several new features aimed at delivering services quickly and efficiently. For example, it allows customers to check in to their hotel, avoiding concierge help desks. If a customer needs assistance, they can request services through the app and receive notifications when requests are complete. The mobile app also eliminates human error by allowing customers to lock and unlock their room door without the need for a troublesome card key.

Marriott has also invested in artificial intelligence to elevate their customer services. Over 5,000 hotels are already using AI-powered chatbots to handle reservation changes, redemption vouchers, and account changes. These features have been further extended to social networks like Facebook, Slack, and WeChat to enable members to connect with hotel concierges, discover local activities, or check room availability.[29]

Marriott envisions a future with smart hotels that address customer needs. They partnered with Samsung to develop full-scale models to test technology that is capable of understanding a customer's preferences and preloading them into the room at check-in. If Marriott can scale this technology, it would mean better personalization options for each customer—something Airbnb couldn't do.[30]

In each of these examples of digital transformation, the adoption and implementation of new technologies have paved the way for company-wide efficiency. Integrating technology to enhance the customer experience allows companies to meet user needs, add more value, and increase revenue growth.

Chapter 7
Delivering Success Through Digital Transformation

Over the years, I've led digital transformation projects for many small and medium-sized companies to large global corporations. My experience has been diverse in working with organizations across high tech, finance, construction, consumer products, industrial engine-eering, packaging and logistics, healthcare, retail, and entertainment industries.

There have been many success stories and lessons learned. In my experience, no two companies are alike. While there are ways to use a standard framework for transformation, it always requires assessing the unique challenges and opportunities for each company to carve out a custom roadmap for their transformation. The tailored approach allows companies to meet their specific business objectives while retaining their DNA and maintaining a competitive edge.

Here are some of the success stories that illustrate how companies across industries and with different needs can overcome challenges through transformation.

DRIVING BUSINESS FORWARD THROUGH AUTOMATION

A few years ago, I met the owner of a leading general contractor. In one of our first conversations he said, "I'm buying 40 iPads and we need to build a mobile app for my team."

"Ok," I replied, "but let's first discuss what we are trying to achieve or solve."

Technology should NEVER be the starting point of business transformation, but rather a mechanism for building or delivering a solution. Companies should focus first on discovering their business problems and growth opportunities.

Delivering Success Through Digital Transformation

This company relied heavily on paper-based processes for handling all of its business. With 500+ employees using manual workflows to manage their daily functions, operational inefficiencies began to surface, which caused delays and cost overruns.

After our initial joint sessions with their team, we determined that they needed a digital solution capable of collecting data, making that data available to different business departments, providing real-time visibility into client projects, and improving collaboration within internal teams and customers. An iPad application alone would not meet those needs, however, creating multiple digital solutions wasn't fiscally possible. To meet their business needs and stay within budget, we built a mobile-friendly cloud application that could be shared by all business departments.

This application converted their lengthy manual process into a seamless and intuitive digital experience, allowing them to manage projects, onboard new clients, complete job orders, complete material orders, manage employees, manage payroll, and access robust reporting data.

It took less than a year to transform their business from paper to digital. This resulted in an average annual cost savings of over $1 million, nearly four times their investment, due to improved project performance and the eradication of manual processes. In addition, digital transformation helped improve the customer experience and delivered 7.5% revenue growth. The company was able to recoup its investment in just a few months.

This is one of my great success stories because it proves that even a small business with no previous technology affiliation could achieve digital transformation. They had commitment from their executive leadership, a willingness from their team to adopt change, a sufficient budget for building a viable digital solution, and an experienced technology partner to make it happen.

IMPROVING CUSTOMER EXPERIENCES THROUGH DATA VISUALIZATION

One of my clients, a software company that provides software solutions to more than 5000 brands across the world, had a technical support team who was remotely managing and supporting customers' software systems. The data gathered from the systems, including errors and health warnings, were kept in databases specific to each customer. The distributed data required technicians to go through multiple layers of data to discover and troubleshoot issues—all of which was slowing down their response times.

To ensure that the customer's business-critical software systems were running optimally, the technical support team had to find ways to improve their response times. To achieve this objective, we partnered with them from design through implementation on a dashboard application that would serve as an access point to all customer data. The development process was highly collaborative and was aided by the clear vision and goals of the technical support team.

The dashboard application significantly reduced the support response times and improved uptime for customer systems. The project, which was completed within a few months, transformed a core process and contributed to the overall success of the business through improved customer retention and reduced support costs by over $10 million annually.

This technology initiative is an excellent example of how a department can take the lead in transforming its processes and make a positive impact on the customer experience and the overall business performance.

"Digital transformation is possible in any organization regardless of its maturity level, size, or industry. All it requires is leadership committed to business growth and a team that is inspired to bring change."

UNITING A GLOBAL CORPORATION THROUGH DIGITAL CONNECTIVITY

In the last 20 years, I've had the opportunity to work with many Fortune 500 companies and large global corporations. Transforming established processes for a global corporation is not an easy undertaking, as business standards tend to vary across different locations and teams. On several occasions, I've come across companies where each department operate in isolation. Even when technology solutions have been implemented, they are managed by separate teams and leadership. A lack of strategic direction and consistency across the business can hurt any company's growth. With the right digital strategy and execution, even the largest business can innovate and start leading other companies within their industry.

A few years ago, a global corporation was experiencing growth challenges and hired us to help with their digital transformation. We began by preparing a corporate digital strategy and a transformation roadmap. We identified processes across departments, gathered business goals, reviewed existing technologies, and defined new solutions. This company was spread across six continents, which meant we had to identify and support different languages, currencies, and timezones as part of our implementation goals. Additionally, we had to define standard practices across departments since this did not already exist within the company.

We divided the company's transformation objectives into multiple digital solutions based on the different business processes, which included solutions for cloud, mobile, and IoT. The proposed digital roadmap took a multi-pronged approach across several years. We started by trans-forming core business functions that immediately improved the work of over 2000 employees supporting over 10,000 customers. These changes also paved the way for new digital solutions that improved collaboration across departments, integrated business applications, and introduced new customer solutions.

Through the process of digital transformation, the DNA of the company evolved into a culture of innovation. New digital solutions increased business revenues by 5% and reduced costs by over 15%, adding over $200 million a year to the business's bottom line. With these innovative solutions, the company found additional business growth opportunities. At the time, this level of transformation wasn't achieved by any other company within their industry, making them a trailblazer and industry-dominating organization.

PUSHING AN INDUSTRY FORWARD THROUGH A DIGITAL PLATFORM

The construction and home building industry is known as one of the most reluctant in implementing digital solutions. While the majority of construction companies are still operating on paper or with very limited use of technology, there are a few that have been transforming their entire business or implementing technology solutions for critical operations.

I've had the opportunity to work with several such companies. One of the most involved experiences required a complete transformation of a construction company, which included everything from sales, project management, vendor management, issue tracking and customer service to accounting, field service, employee tracking, and back-office operations.

Building digital solutions for this company presented some unique challenges. There was no standardization for business processes and data, so we had to come up with the best practices. Many of the employees were apprehensive about using software applications, and we had to ensure that the user experience of the new systems supported the onboarding of non-technical employees. Historical data was critical for business. With that, we had to find ways to migrate data from legacy systems into the new systems and import non-digital data into the new systems, as well. To achieve full automation, new systems had to be integrated with their ERP software.

As the new systems were built, they were piloted with a small number of users before rolling out across the company's entire business of over 300,000 employees, vendors, and customers. The implementation strategy helped us test the new systems within a limited scope to collect feedback and perfect the systems before its release. The testing also helped identify power users who easily adopted to the new processes and systems, and also be tapped to onboard other users for a smoother transition.

While the full transformation was achieved over several years, it made a lasting impact, exceeding business goals. Automation helped the company lower production costs, improve construction quality, establish employee accountability, and forecast market trends. The company earned 10 times its initial technology investments within the first year of launch and improved profitability by over $250 million in less than five years.

Through transformation and automation, companies can achieve breakout performance, regardless of the technology adoption within their business or industry. The development of complex enterprise solutions requires a significant commitment from leadership, and strong performance by the technology team. In the end, the dramatically positive results make the investment a worthwhile endeavor.

In the digital age, the only way to survive and thrive is to embrace digital

————

Conclusion

Digital transformation is less about technology and more about your business strategy. **It's about your people, your process, and your data.** How do you change your work culture so that your employees collaborate better, become more productive, and start innovating? How do you refine existing processes to streamline workflows, improve customer experiences, and create new opportunities? How do you gather data specific to your operations and your customers to measure performance, forecast trends, and improve products?

In order to thrive in the digital age, organizations need leadership that can lead their transformation through innovation. They need to change existing business models, introduce new products and services, and guide the entire team through the process. Digital transformation is not just for larger enterprises; small and medium-sized businesses also need to transform digitally to stay competitive and scale operations for further growth.

Digital transformation requires strategic thinking. You cannot implement technology without understanding its real value for your business. For a successful transformation, you must create a digital roadmap and use it as a guiding principle. Your team's readiness to support business objectives and foster a culture of innovation is crucial for meeting your goals.

New digital technologies are advancing at a fast pace, which makes it difficult for most organizations to maintain in-house resources with the required skills. Many organizations are testing new technologies for business value. Don't be left out. While it may seem like a massive undertaking, you don't have to take on a digital transformation alone. Rely on technology partners to help you address your specific needs and to accelerate your transformation.

Digital transformation is not an overnight change, but rather an ongoing journey that continues as digital technologies advance and business needs evolve. By building a strategic roadmap and starting with small changes, you can slowly begin to transform key areas of the business and eventually be successful in meeting all objectives.

Measuring results from your digital transformation is essential. Establishing benchmarks can help you measure the actual benefits received against the forecasted goals. How well is the user adoption of new digital tools? Are you able to cut down on mundane tasks and improve operational efficiency? Are revenues growing at a faster rate? Has the overall brand perception in the industry improved? Has the average customer retention increased? Are your employees happier? Measuring outcome from your digital transformation and tackling problems early on can help you achieve better returns from your investments.

Risks of not adopting digital can be significant. You will continue to face growing competition from the digital-savvy competitors and digital startups in your industry. In the digital age, the only way to survive and thrive is to embrace digital.

Digital Transformation Worksheet

Digital transformation is a strategic business initiative that requires a new way of looking at existing business models and defining changes. These worksheet questions will help you reflect on the current state of your business, determine its readiness for the transformation, and help define your transformative goals.

1. What are my digital transformation objectives?

2. What digital solutions can improve my employees' working environment?

3. What digital solutions can help improve relationships with my customers?

4. What individual or team will lead my digital transformation?

5. What skills will my team need to deliver digital initiatives?

6. Do I need outside expertise for some or all of my digital initiatives?

7. How will I document feedback from my digital initiatives?

8. What criteria will I use for measuring the results of digital transformation?

Endnotes

1. Eileen Smith, "Worldwide Spending on Digital Transformation Will Be Nearly $2 Trillion in 2022 as Organizations Commit to DX, According to a New IDC Spending Guide", *IDC*, November 13, 2018, https://www.idc.com/getdoc.jsp?containerId=prUS44440318

2. Robert William, "Domino's lets AI assistant 'Dom' handle incoming phone orders," *Mobile Marketer*, April 25, 2018, https://www.mobilemarketer.com/news/dominos-lets-ai-assistant-dom-handle-incoming-phone-orders/522111/

3. DST Kasina, "Putnam Investments ranked #1 for digital engagement with financial advisors", *Putnam Investments*, October 31, 2016, https://www.putnam. com/newsroom/press-release/150-putnam-investments-ranked-1-for-digital-en-gagement-with-financial-advisors

4. "CEMEX Go Reaches 20K Customers in 18 Countries Within First Year", *Cemex*, November

6, 2018, https://www.cemexusa.com/-/cemex-go-reaches-20k-customers-in-18-countries-within-first-year

5. "Here's A List Of 68 Bankruptcies In The Retail Apocalypse And Why They Failed", *CB Insights*, March 12, 2019, https://www.cbinsights.com/research/ retail-apocalypse-timeline-infographic/

6. "Why transformations fail: A conversation with Seth Goldstrom", McKinsey, February 2019, https://www.mckinsey.com/business-functions/ strategy-and-corporate-finance/our-insights/why-transformations-fail-a-conver-sation-with-seth-goldstrom

7. Simon Kemp, "Digital 2019: Global Internet Use Accelerates", We Are Social, January 30, 2019, https://wearesocial.com/blog/2019/01/digi-tal-2019-global-internet-use-accelerates

8. "2011 Customer Experience Impact Report", *Oracle Corporation*, 2011, http://www.oracle.com/us/products/applicati ons/cust-exp-impact-report-epss-1560493.pdf

9. Matthew Johnsen, "3 Top Data Challenges And How Firms Solved Them", *IBM* September 19, 2018,

https://www.ibmbigdatahub.com/blog/3-top-data-chal-lenges-and-how-firms-solved-them

10. Joao Marques Lima, "Enterprises Are Wasting $140bn With Data Trapped In Legacy Systems", *Data Economy*, June 27, 2017, https://data-economy.com/ enterprises-wasting-140bn-data-trapped-legacy-systems/

11. "Benefits of Cloud Computing", *IBM*, May 09, 2019, https://www.ibm.com/cloud/learn/benefits-of-cloud-computing

12. Janaki Akella, Brad Brown, Greg Gilbert, Lawrence Wong, "Mobility Disrup-tion: A CIO Perspective", *McKinsey*, September 2012, https://www.mckinsey.com/ business-functions/mckinsey-digital/our-insights/mobility-disruption-a-cio-per-spective

13. Mark Hung, "Leading The IoT", *Gartner*, 2017, https://www.gartner.com/imagesrv/books/iot/iotEbook_digital.pdf

14. Tanguy Catlin, Johannes-Tobias Lorenz, Bob Sternfels, and Paul Willmott, "A roadmap for digital transformation", *McKinsey*, March 2017, https://www.mckinsey.com/industries/financial-

services/our-insights/a-roadmap-for-a-digi-
tal-transformation

15. "Selling Digital Transformation In Your
    Enterprise", Daniel Newman, *CMO Network*,
    March 21, 2017,
    https://www.forbes.com/sites/danielnew-
    man/2017/03/21/selling-digital-
    transformation-in-your-
    enterprise/#106ff5fe697f

16. Mark Samuels, "What Is A Chief Digital Officer",
    ZDNet, December 21, 2018,
    https://www.zdnet.com/article/what-is-a-
    chief-digital-officer-everything-you-need-to-
    know-about-the-cdo/

17. Ben Wigert and Jennifer Robison, "Fostering
    Creativity at Work: Do Your Managers Push or
    Crush Innovation?", *Gallup*, December 19, 2018,
    https://www.gallup.com/workplace/245498/f
    ostering-creativity-work-manag-ers-push-
    crush-innovation.aspx

18. Bob Evans, "Inside Walmart's Digital
    Transformation: 30 Tangible Steps on its
    Journey", *Cloud Wars,* February 22, 2019,
    https://cloudwars.co/ inside-walmart-digital-
    transformation/

Endnotes

19. Jane Incao, "How VR is Transforming the Way We Train Associates", *Walmart*, September 20, 2018, https://corporate.walmart.com/newsroom/innova-tion/20180920/how-vr-is-transforming-the-way-we-train-associates

20. "Walmart Online sales rise 37% in Q1", *Digital Commerce 360*, May 16, 2019, https://www.digitalcommerce360.com/2019/05/16/walmarts-online-sales-rise-37-in-q1/

21. Lance Murray, "Best Buy CEO Outlines 5-Point Plan to Renew Blue", *BizJournals*, November 13, 2012, https://www.bizjournals.com/dallas/news/2012/11/13/best-buy-ceo-outlines-5-point-plan-to.html

22. "Best Buy Fiscal Year 2018 Corporate Responsibility & Sustainability Report", *Best Buy*, 2018, https://corporate.bestbuy.com/wp-content/ uploads/2018/06/FY18-full-report-FINAL.pdf

23. Yoel Minkoff, "Best Buy sees $50B in revenue, $1B in cost savings by 2025", *Seeking Alpha*, September 25, 2019, https://seekingalpha.com/ news/3501654-best-buy-sees-50b-revenue-1b-cost-savings-2025

24. "Weight Watchers Accelerates Digital Transformation With LightBend", *Lightbend*, 2019, https://www.lightbend.com/case-studies/weight-watchers-ac-celerates-digital-transformation-with-lightbend

25. "WW App Wins Webby Award and People's Voice Webby Award in "Apps, Mobile, and Voice: Best Practices" Category", *Weight Watchers*, April 23, 2019, https://www.prnewswire.com/news-releases/ww-app-wins-webby-award-and-peoples-voice-webby-award-in-apps-mobile-and-voice-best-practices-cate-gory-300836727.html

26. Stephanie Condon, "WW, Formerly Weight Watchers, launches new voice app", *ZDNet*, March 19, 2019, https://www.zdnet.com/article/ww-formerly-weight-watchers-launches-new-voice-app/

27. Alok Shah, "StubHub Finds Ticket to Effective Digital Asset Management with Cloudinary", *Cloudinary*, May 28, 2019, https://cloudinary.com/blog/stubhub_finds_ticket_to_effective_digital_asset_management_with_cloudinary

28. Nicole Lee, "StubHub app uses VR to show how good (or bad) your seats are", *Engadget*, March 31, 2016, https://www.engadget.com/2016/03/31/stub hub-app-uses-vr-to-show-how-good-or-bad-your-seats-are/

29. "Marriot Mobile App", *Marriot Bonvoy*, 2019, https://mobileapp.marriott. com/#

30. "Marriott International Teams With Samsung And Legrand To Unveil Hospi-tality Industry's IoT Hotel Room Of The Future, Enabling The Company To Deepen Personalized Guest Experience", *Marriott International, Inc.*, November 14, 2017, https://www.prnewswire.com/news-releases/marriott-international-teams-with-samsung-and-legrand-to-unveil-hospitality-industrys iot-hotel-room-of-the-future-enabling-the-company-to-deepen-personalized-guest-experience-300555659.html

About The Author

Maulik Shah is CEO of technology consulting company Invonto. He is a business-savvy technologist with over 20 years of industry experience. He advises his clients on digital strategy and has led several digital initiatives for companies such as Transamerica, Pulte Homes, D. R. Horton, Epicor, EY, Sealed Air, YMCA, Columbus McKinnon, West, Bottomline Technologies, and Southco. He is often featured in digital and print publications for his views on technology trends, entrepreneurship, American workforce, and digital transformation. He holds a master's degree in Computer Science.

About Invonto

Invonto is an American technology consulting company providing digital transformation solutions to many small businesses, Fortune 500 companies, and large global corporations. Invonto develops digital solutions for cloud, mobile, Internet of Things (IoT), augmented reality, virtual reality, and Artificial Intelligence (AI). Digital solutions built by Invonto team has helped clients transform legacy systems, automate business processes, improve employee experiences, and strengthen client relationships. Since 2008, Invonto's team has built turn-key solutions that have generated over $2.5 billion in revenue growth for companies in the high tech, finance, construction, retail, consumer products, industrial engineering, pharma, healthcare, and entertainment industries.

www.invonto.com

Made in the USA
Middletown, DE
23 December 2019

81623224R00070